Contents

3

Create Viral TikTok Videos And Build Your Audience

Strategies to Master TikTok and Grow Your Followers

Nova Johansson

2024

Legal Notice

Disclaimer

About This Book

This book is designed to be your comprehensive roadmap to success on TikTok, offering a mix of creative strategies, practical tips, and actionable insights that effectively can be used by both newcomers and experienced creators. Whether you're an aspiring influencer, a business looking to amplify your brand, or simply curious about the platform's unique dynamics, this book equips you with the understanding of trends, strategies and tools you need to thrive.

This book is the result of trial and error, observing what types of content truly resonate with audiences on TikTok. Through these insights, I want to help you skip the guesswork and start creating impactful videos that not only capture attention but have the potential to go viral, no matter the size of your current following.

What This Book Offers

This book will take you through the 10 essential steps and actions needed to create content that has the potential to go viral. From understanding the fundamentals of the TikTok algorithm to leveraging humour, visual cues, and trends effectively. Each chapter provides you with practical tips and proven strategies to help you succeed on the platform.

Whether you're a beginner looking to grow your presence or an experienced creator aiming to refine your approach, this guide will provide you with the tools and knowledge you need to create TikTok videos that not only capture attention but also foster genuine engagement and growth.

What You'll Learn

Take Advantage of Trends and Algorithms: Understand how to identify and capitalize on emerging trends quickly. You'll learn the ins and outs of TikTok's algorithm and how to use it to your advantage.

Crafting Engaging Content: Discover techniques for creating videos that resonate with your audience, from using humour and relatability to mastering visual storytelling.

Developing a Consistent Strategy: Learn how to balance quality and frequency in your posting strategy, ensuring your content is both engaging and consistent.

Building on Viral Success: Find out how to maintain momentum after a viral hit, spinning new ideas and engaging with your audience to keep the buzz alive.

Navigating TikTok's Features: How to effectively create captivating hooks, you'll explore the platform's features and how to leverage them for maximum reach and engagement.

Utilizing AI for Scriptwriting: Explore how to use tools like ChatGPT to generate compelling scripts, refine your ideas and streamline the content process.

How This Book is Structured

Each chapter delves into a specific aspect of content creation on TikTok, offering detailed explanations, real-world examples, and step-by-step instructions. You'll find practical advice on everything from crafting effective hooks and engaging with your community to using AI for scriptwriting and capitalizing on viral moments. Throughout the book, you'll be guided on how to turn insights into action, empowering you to create compelling content that captures attention and builds a loyal following.

To help you apply each concept to your own creative journey, each chapter ends with "Content Creation Boosters" thought-provoking and practical exercises designed to spark new ideas and get you started with your content creation. These boosters will inspire you to reflect on the strategies discussed and personalize them for your unique style and goals. By the end of this book, you'll have a deep understanding of what it takes to create viral TikTok videos and establish a strong presence on the platform.

About the Author

I Nova Johansson am a digital creator, e-commerce strategist, and marketing expert with over 20 years of experience in driving growth and innovation in the digital space. Throughout my career, I've taken a hands-on approach to online marketing, social media strategy and e-commerce.

With a strong foundation in online services and customer acquisition, I've successfully navigated the evolving landscape of digital marketing. My expertise spans SEO, branding, and developing impactful social media campaigns. I've led projects that significantly increased brand visibility, enhanced customer engagement, and fueled business growth, adapting to the dynamic changes in the digital world.

My passion for understanding the mechanics of viral content has driven me to experiment extensively on TikTok, where I've generated millions of views through creative and effective strategies. These experiments weren't just about achieving numbers, they were about uncovering the principles that make content resonate and spread organically.

After three years of experimenting with TikTok, analysing countless clips, and testing various strategies to understand the platform's algorithm, I decided to compile my findings into this book. My goal is to create a comprehensive guide that not only explains how the TikTok algorithm works but also provides actionable steps for creating content that maximizes engagement.

Introduction

Unleashing the Power of TikTok

One of TikTok's most unique features is that it gives every video a fair chance to go viral, regardless of the creator's follower count. Unlike other social media platforms where reach is often determined by the size of your audience, TikTok ensures that even brand-new accounts or those with few followers can capture millions of views. The algorithm measures engagement on individual clips such as likes, shares, and watch time and promotes content based on its performance rather than the creator's popularity. This democratized approach to virality is what makes TikTok stand out in the social media landscape and why it has become a platform where anyone can potentially achieve viral success.

Understanding TikTok's Algorithm

The TikTok algorithm, designed to serve users highly engaging content, offers an unprecedented opportunity for creators to go viral even those with no prior following. Unlike other social media platforms, where reach is often tied to follower count, TikTok democratizes virality, allowing any video to potentially reach millions. This unique aspect has transformed TikTok into a cultural phenomenon and a powerful launchpad for creators, brands, and influencers to reach new audiences in ways that were unimaginable just a few years ago.

The Power of Trends

Central to TikTok's success is its trend-driven culture. Trends on TikTok can range from viral challenges and hashtag movements to catchy audio clips and memes. Riding the wave of a trending topic can catapult a video into the limelight, gaining immense visibility and engagement in a matter of hours. However, creating viral content requires more than just jumping on a trend, it demands a strategic blend of creativity, timing, and authenticity.

Understanding the TikTok Algorithm

The TikTok algorithm is a sophisticated system that determines which videos are shown to users on their "For You" page (FYP). Unlike other platforms, TikTok's algorithm offers a unique opportunity for anyone regardless of follower count to go viral. Understanding how it works can significantly boost your chances of success.

The TikTok algorithm is a powerful tool that, when understood and utilized correctly, can help you reach a vast audience. By focusing on creating engaging content, leveraging trending elements, and maintaining consistency, you can significantly increase your chances of success on the platform.

Analyse your own performance regularly. Use TikTok's analytics to understand what's working and refine your strategy based on what resonates with your audience. Remember that TikTok rewards creativity and engagement. Focus on delivering value in your videos, whether through entertainment, education, or inspiration, to keep viewers coming back for more.

Here follows in short how the TikTok algorithm is working and we will dig deeper into each of the areas along the book.

How the Algorithm Works

The algorithm is designed to deliver a personalized content experience to every user. It considers several key factors:

User Interactions: This includes the videos you like, share, comment on, and the accounts you follow. The more you interact with certain types of content, the more the algorithm will show similar videos.

Video Information: Elements like captions, hashtags, and sounds used in your video are crucial. The algorithm scans this data to understand what your video is about and who might be interested in it.

Device and Account Settings: Information like your language preference, location, and device type can influence what you see, though these are less weighted than other factors.

Watch Time and Engagement: One of the most critical factors is how much time users spend watching your video. High watch time and strong engagement (likes, shares, comments) signal to the algorithm that your content is worth promoting.

Breaking Down the Key Factors

Crafting Content that Connects

Likes and Comments: Engage with your audience by prompting them to like and comment. Ask questions or include a call-to-action in your video.

Shares: Encourage viewers to share your video with friends. Content that sparks a reaction or emotion is more likely to be shared.

Follows: Make it easy for viewers to follow you by including a clear call-to-action at the end of your videos. This signals to the algorithm that you are producing valuable and professional content.

Use Hashtags, Sounds, and Captions

Hashtags: Use relevant and trending hashtags to categorize your content. Include a mix of broad and niche hashtags to increase discoverability.

Sounds: Popular sounds are often pushed by the algorithm. Incorporate trending music or sound effects in your videos to increase the chances of being featured on the FYP.

Captions: Use engaging captions that include keywords related to your video. This helps the algorithm understand your content better.

Watch Time and Replays

Hook Your Audience Early: The first 2-3 seconds of your video are critical. Use engaging visuals or compelling statements to capture attention immediately. Shorter videos (under 15 seconds) are more likely to be watched in full, increasing your watch time ratio. This signals to the algorithm that your content is engaging.

Encourage Replays: Create content that viewers will want to watch multiple times. This could be a clever loop, a surprise twist, or intricate details that aren't obvious at first glance.

Common Myths About the Algorithm

"You Need a Large Following to Go Viral": TikTok's algorithm is designed to showcase content that is engaging, regardless of the creator's follower count. Even new accounts can have viral videos if they engage viewers effectively.

"Only the First Few Videos Get Views": While the algorithm may give a small boost to new accounts to help them gain traction, this does not mean older accounts can't go viral. Consistent, high-quality content can achieve virality at any time.

"Deleting Videos Hurts Your Reach": There is no evidence that deleting videos affects your overall reach. If a video isn't performing well, it's okay to remove it and try a different approach.

ACTION 1
SPEED IS KEY
JUMP ON TRENDS
QUICKLY

What You Will Learn

- SPEED IS KEY •
- TRENDS HAVE SHORT LIFESPANS •
- MONITOR TRENDING SOUNDS AND HASHTAGS •
- FOCUS ON RELEVANCE OVER PERFECTION •
- LEVERAGE THIRD-PARTY TOOLS •

Action 1 -
Speed is Key
Jump on Trends Quickly

Why Speed is Crucial for Viral Success

Trends on TikTok move at lightning speed. What's popular today might be forgotten tomorrow, so the ability to create and post content quickly is essential. When you are among the first to engage with a trend, you benefit from less competition and higher visibility. This increases the chances of your video being featured on the "For You" page while the trend is still gaining traction.

Early Movers Advantage

The TikTok algorithm favours videos that capture attention quickly. If your video gains views, likes, and comments rapidly after posting, the algorithm interprets this as a signal of high-quality content and will push it to a broader audience. Posting early ensures you get this initial boost when competition is minimal.

Capitalizing on Fresh Trends

When a trend is fresh, users are more likely to explore new content related to it. This means your video is more likely to be discovered by users actively seeking out new takes on the trending topic. If you wait too long, the trend becomes saturated, and your video may struggle to stand out.

Identify Emerging Trends Quickly

Trend Tools

Use TikTok's "Discover" page to find trending hashtags and sounds. Follow popular creators in your niche who often set or ride trends. You can also track other social platforms and news to spot trends before they hit TikTok.

Advanced Trend Tracking

Consider using third-party tools like TrendTok or Google Trends to monitor keywords and hashtags related to your niche. This will help you act early when new trends emerge.

Create Videos at the Speed of Trends

Simple is Better

Viral content doesn't need to be overly complex. Focus on simple, fast execution. You can use the in-app editor to shoot, add music, and post quickly. It's more important to be fast and relevant than perfect.

Planning Ahead

Stay ready by having a content plan. If a trend related to your niche emerges, you can jump on it without hesitation. Maintain a high content distribution so you can pivot to trending topics as needed.

Fast Content Creation

Batch Recording

Record multiple clips in one session so you have content ready to edit and post as trends emerge. This allows for faster posting without scrambling for fresh footage.

Reuse and Repurpose

Don't be afraid to reuse content, remix older posts, or react to your own videos to stay relevant and post quickly.

Action Tip: Keep your video creation process agile and focused. When a new trend appears, aim to create and post within hours. Prioritize relevance over perfection to catch the wave before it fades.

Strategy Insight: Being one of the first to jump on a trend dramatically increases your chances of going viral. TikTok's algorithm favours early movers, and even a simple, quickly made video can gain millions of views if it's timely.

Content Creation Boosters

Identify a Trending Hashtag Today
Open TikTok's Discover page and pick one trending hashtag that aligns with your content niche. How could you create a quick video around this trend? Brainstorm a 15-second video idea that you can produce and upload today.

Set a 24-Hour Trend Challenge
Select a recent news event or pop culture moment that you think is gaining traction. Create a plan to produce a video based on this topic within the next 24 hours. How will you incorporate trending audio or visuals to make it relevant?

Speed Over Perfection
Take a look at your content queue or ideas list. Choose one concept that's not fully polished and challenge yourself to create and post it within a couple of hours. Reflect: How does this "imperfect" content perform compared to your more polished videos?

Monitor Hashtag Growth
Use a third-party trend-tracking tool like TrendTok or TikTok's own analytics to monitor the rise of hashtags in your niche. After identifying a fast-growing hashtag, brainstorm how you can create content around it this week.

Build a Trend Library
Start compiling a list of trends, popular sounds, or challenges you've noticed over the last week. For each, write down a quick idea for how you could jump on that trend quickly, then keep this as a reference for future content planning.

ACTION 2
PRIORITIZE
RELEVANCE
OVER PERFECTION

What You Will Learn

- POSTING TIMELY • RELATING TO TRENDS •
- FAST EXECUTION MATTERS •
- MAXIMIZING ENGAGEMENT •
- PERFECTION CAN BE A BARRIER •

Action 2 –
Prioritize Relevance Over Perfection

Why Relevance Trumps Perfection

On TikTok, the speed at which you create and post content can often be more important than achieving perfect production quality. The platform thrives on timely, relatable content that speaks directly to current trends and audience interests. Focusing on perfection can lead to delays, missing the peak of a trend or conversation.

Timely Content

TikTok's algorithm rewards videos that engage with ongoing trends and discussions. If you wait too long to perfect your video, the moment may pass, and the opportunity for high engagement can be lost.

Authenticity Over Polish

Users on TikTok appreciate authenticity and spontaneity. Unlike platforms that may favour polished, highly-produced content, TikTok thrives on real, relatable moments. Being authentic can resonate more deeply with your audience than a meticulously edited video.

How to Create Relevant Content Quickly

Identify Trending Topics

Regularly check TikTok's "Discover" page and keep an eye on trending hashtags, challenges, and sounds. This will give you an idea of what's currently engaging the platform's users.

Simplify Your Process

Develop a streamlined content creation process. For example, create templates for common video types or use pre-set filters and effects to save time.

Leverage Your Own Style

Use your unique voice or perspective to participate in trends. Adding a personal twist to popular topics makes your content stand out without sacrificing timeliness.

Best Practices for Relevant Content Creation

Batch Create Content

Record several short clips in one session. This way, you have content ready to post at a fixed schedule, letting you take advantage of one scene for many purposes.

Use Remixes and Duets

Engage with other creators' content through remixes or duets. This allows you to add your perspective to trending videos without having to create something from scratch.

Engage in Real-Time

Respond to comments and interact with viewers as soon as you post. This real-time engagement can boost your video's performance and help it gain traction faster.

Examples of Relevance Over Perfection

Quick Reactions

A creator sees a news story trending and immediately posts a short, unedited reaction video. The content is timely and authentic, gaining thousands of views even though the production is minimal.

Participation in Challenges

Instead of overthinking choreography or set design for a trending dance challenge, a creator films a quick video in their living room. The casual setting makes the video relatable and connects with the audience on a personal level.

Action Tip: Set a goal to create and post content within a tight timeframe and aim for no more than 30 minutes from idea to upload. This will help you focus on relevance and keep up with fast-moving trends.

Strategy Insight: Remember, TikTok users are more likely to engage with content that feels authentic and timely rather than polished but detached. By prioritizing relevance, you increase your chances of reaching a broader audience and becoming part of trending conversations.

Content Creation Boosters

Jump on a Current Trend

Identify a trending topic or event that's relevant to your niche. Create a short video today that adds your perspective or a unique twist to this trend. Focus on posting quickly rather than perfecting every detail.

Analyse Trending Videos

Spend 10 minutes scrolling through TikTok's "For You Page." Note three trending videos in your niche and identify what makes them timely and relevant. How can you create something similar but with your own spin?

Set a Speed Challenge

Challenge yourself to create a video in less than 30 minutes based on a current event or trend. The goal is to prioritize getting it out quickly while it's still relevant. How does this approach feel compared to your usual process?

Refine Your Trending Topics Strategy

Make a list of trends that often occur in your niche. Keep this list handy, and the next time a similar topic arises, use it as a blueprint to post fast without worrying about perfection.

Create a "Good Enough" Video

Choose a video idea that you've been sitting on because it's not fully polished. Give yourself a deadline to finish and post it as is. Did it perform better or worse than your more perfected content?

ACTION 3
LEVERAGE
HUMOUR AND
RELATABILITY

What You Will Learn

- USE HUMOR TO CONNECT •
- BALANCE FUN WITH VALUE •
- HIGHLIGHT EVERYDAY SITUATIONS •
- EXAGGERATE FOR EFFECT •
- INCORPORATE TRENDS •

Action 3 – Leverage Humour and Relatability

Humour is a powerful tool on TikTok. It transcends different niches and topics, making your content more engaging and shareable. Even serious subjects, like technology or business, can benefit from a touch of humour to break down complex ideas and make them more accessible and relatable. People are more likely to engage with and share content that makes them smile or laugh, which helps increase visibility and reach.

Finding Humour in Everyday Situations

Humour often lies in the ordinary, everyday moments that we can all relate to. Whether it's a funny mishap at work, a relatable struggle in daily life, or an ironic twist on common scenarios, highlighting these moments in your videos can create an instant connection with your audience.

Think about situations like technical glitches, work-from-home struggles, or awkward Zoom meetings. Exaggerate these scenarios or put a humorous spin on them to make them more engaging.

Action Tip: Use self-deprecating humour or poke fun at common frustrations. This makes your content feel more authentic and allows viewers to see a more human side of you.

Injecting Humour into Serious Topics

Even serious or technical subjects can benefit from a humorous approach. When discussing complex topics, humour can make the information more digestible and engaging.

If you're talking about a tech issue, you could frame it as an over-the-top disaster, like "The time I almost broke the internet trying to fix my Wi-Fi." For finance, you might joke about "the struggle of budgeting vs. the urge to buy one more gadget."

Action Tip: Use visual comedy, like exaggerated facial expressions or props to illustrate your points. For instance, using dramatic acts or memes can add a light-hearted touch to otherwise dry content.

Building Relatability Through Personal Stories

Sharing personal anecdotes or stories that your audience can relate to builds a sense of connection and community. When viewers see their own experiences reflected in your content, they are more likely to engage and share.

If you've experienced a common issue like "accidentally sending a text to the wrong person," share your story in a funny, over-the-top way. This not only entertains but also invites viewers to share their similar experiences.

Action Tip: Identify what's inherently funny or ironic about a situation and build your content around that hook. For example, if you're creating a video about a complex tech problem, exaggerate the confusion or the dramatic "solution" to make it humorous and engaging.

Strategy Insight: Humour and relatability make your content more shareable. When viewers see themselves in your stories or laugh at your jokes, they're more likely to interact with your content, leave comments, and share it with their friends boosting your visibility and reach on TikTok.

Content Creation Boosters

Turn a Common Problem into a Joke

Think of a frustrating or relatable situation that your audience often experiences. How can you turn this into a humorous scenario for a TikTok video? Focus on exaggerating the emotions or reactions to make it funnier.

Experiment with Self-Deprecating Humour

Create a video where you poke fun at yourself in a relatable way. Whether it's a mistake you made or a common challenge in your niche, show your audience that you don't take yourself too seriously.

Observe Everyday Situations for Comedy

Take a moment to observe something in your daily life that could be made into a funny TikTok. It could be an interaction with technology, a pet, or a typical daily struggle. Create a quick video turning that moment into a humorous skit.

Use Trending Sounds to Add Humour

Pick a trending sound on TikTok and apply it in an unexpected, humorous way. Take a serious subject from your niche and pair it with the sound for a comedic twist.

Create a Character or Persona

Develop a character based on a stereotype or exaggerated traits in your niche (e.g., the overly confident "tech expert" or the stressed-out entrepreneur). How can you use this character to make everyday situations funny and relatable?

ACTION 4
USE VISUAL
CUES AND HOOKS
TO GRAB ATTENTION

What You Will Learn

· GRAB ATTENTION INSTANTLY · CREATE A STRONG HOOK ·
· USE PROPS AND DYNAMIC VISUALS ·
· SET THE TONE QUICKLY ·
· EXPERIMENT WITH BOLD ELEMENTS ·

Action 4 –
Use Visual Cues and Hooks to Grab Attention

Capturing attention within the first few seconds of your TikTok video is crucial. With so much content available, you need to make a strong impression right away to prevent viewers from scrolling past. Both visual cues and hooks are essential tools for achieving this, each serving a unique purpose in engaging your audience.

Why Visual Cues and Hooks Matter

TikTok's format is designed for rapid consumption, with users often deciding whether to continue watching a video within the first 2-3 seconds. Effective visual cues and hooks can help you capture interest quickly, communicate your message clearly, and set the tone for what viewers can expect.

Grab Attention Instantly

Bright colours, unexpected scenes, or unusual props can surprise viewers and make them pause. The element of surprise or curiosity is key in convincing them to watch more.

Set the Tone Quickly

Your visuals and hooks should immediately convey what the video is about, helping viewers decide whether it's content they want to engage with.

Understanding the Difference Between Hooks and Visual Cues

The Hook

Capturing initial interest the hook is your opening statement something that grabs attention right from the start and makes viewers want to keep watching. It can be a visual, auditory, or combined element that introduces the main idea of your video. The hook's goal is to capture immediate interest and curiosity. It tells viewers what the video is about or teases an intriguing reveal.

Visual Hook

A dramatic visual, like spilling a cup of coffee over a laptop. Requires just one second of the most dramatic part of the clip.

Audible Hook

A compelling question like, "Ever wonder why this happens?" or a surprising statement like, "This simple trick saved me $500!"

Visual Cues

Guiding and maintaining attention visual cues are elements within the video that guide the viewer's focus and emphasize important parts of your content. They can be used throughout the video to enhance understanding, highlight key points or add emphasis. Visual cues support the hook by keeping the viewer engaged and directing attention to specific details throughout the video.

Strategy Insight

To create engaging and dynamic TikTok videos, consider incorporating text overlays to highlight key phrases or statistics that grab attention. Use quick cuts and zooms to shift camera angles or zoom in on crucial details, emphasizing important moments in your video. Additionally, filming in unique locations or using props can visually enhance your message, making the content more intriguing and shareable.

Action Tip: Combine a strong hook with compelling visual cues. Start with a striking image or bold statement to hook viewers and use visual cues to sustain their interest and highlight key messages.

Using Bold Visual Elements Effectively

When using visual cues, think about how you can exaggerate or highlight key elements of your story or message. Incorporate props, dynamic movements, and unique settings to create an engaging visual narrative that supports your hook.

Props and Settings

Use props or settings that are eye-catching and unusual. For instance, filming a serious topic in a humorous or unexpected location, like discussing productivity tips while riding a roller-coaster.

Dynamic Movements

Quick movements transitions and camera angles can add energy and excitement. Experiment with different shots to keep the visual flow dynamic and engaging.

Strategy Insight: A creator starts a video with an exaggerated scene, such as pretending to have a serious meeting while sitting in a pool. This unusual setup piques curiosity and compels viewers to keep watching to see what happens next.

Creating a Visually Engaging Setup

Design the opening scene of your video with eye-catching elements that hint at what's to come. Consider visuals that will make viewers stop and think, "What's going on here?" This might involve using bright colours, surprising movements, or creative use of space.

Start with a Hook: Use a visually striking or un-expected image in the first frame. This could be something funny, surprising, or mysterious that encourages viewers to stay and watch.

Keep It Simple: While it's important to grab attention, don't overload the frame with too much visual information. Focus on one or two key elements that stand out.

Action Tip: Plan your opening shot carefully. Choose props, settings, or movements that are unexpected and visually appealing to create an immediate hook that stops viewers from scrolling past.

Strategy Insight: Visual cues and hooks work together to enhance your content. The hook draws viewers in, while visual cues guide them through the video, keeping them engaged and interested. Using both effectively can increase your video's chances of being shared and going viral.

Content Creation Boosters

Create a Strong Hook the First 2 Seconds

Think about how you can grab attention visually within the first 2 seconds of your next video. Use bright colours, unexpected movements, or exaggerated expressions. Test this with a quick video and see how the hook affects your viewer retention.

Incorporate Bold Props or Settings

Choose one prop (like oversized glasses or a surprising object) or an unusual setting (e.g., a bathroom or rooftop) to make your video visually stand out. Use it in your opening shot to intrigue viewers and keep them watching.

Use Quick Transitions for Dynamic Energy

Film a video where you use rapid transitions between scenes or angles to keep the viewer engaged. Try using jump cuts or quick pans that change the perspective often. How does this technique affect the pacing and energy of your video?

Design a Scene with an Element of Surprise

Plan a scene where something unexpected happens visually. It could be something like throwing a pile of papers, a costume change, or an object that "comes to life." Capture this moment within the first few seconds of your video to hook viewers.

Focus on a Visual Story

Create a video that tells a story visually without relying heavily on text or audio. Use movements, expressions, and props to guide the narrative. After posting, reflect on how well the visual storytelling alone held viewers' attention.

ACTION 5
POST CONSISTENTLY
AND BUILD
MOMENTUM

What You Will Learn

- DEVELOP A POSTING SCHEDULE •
- EXPERIMENT AND REFINE • LEVERAGE ANALYTICS •
- CONSISTENCY DRIVES GROWTH •
- QUANTITY OVER PERFECTION •

Action 5 –
Post Consistently and
Build Momentum

Consistency in posting is crucial for building a strong presence on TikTok and posting regularly increases your chances of hitting virality. Even if not every video goes viral, regularly uploading content helps maintain visibility and fosters audience growth. However, consistency goes beyond just posting frequently it's also about creating a cohesive look and feel for your profile.

Why Consistency Matters

Regular posting increases your chances of being seen by more people, as TikTok's algorithm favours active accounts. Consistency also helps build anticipation and trust with your audience, making them more likely to follow and engage with your content.

Boosts Algorithmic Favor

The more you post, the more likely the algorithm is to push your videos to the "For You" page. Even if some videos don't perform well, your active status can still increase your overall visibility.

Audience Retention

Consistent content keeps your audience engaged and coming back for more. Viewers are more likely to follow accounts that regularly provide value, entertainment, or updates.

Keep a Consistent Posting Schedule

Establishing a regular posting schedule is key to staying on track without compromising content quality. Use batch creation and scheduling tools to maintain a steady flow of content, even during busy periods.

Daily Posts: Aim to post once a day. It's not about every video being a hit but about maintaining a consistent presence.

Batch Creation: Record multiple videos in one sitting and save them to post over the coming days. This helps you stay consistent even if you can't create content daily.

Experimenting with Different Content

Not every video needs to be a major production. Mix up your content to keep things interesting for your audience and to prevent burnout.

Short Updates: Share quick thoughts, day-in-the-life clips, or short reactions to trends. These can be easy to produce and still engage your audience.

Interactive Content: Use features like Q&A, polls, or duets to involve your audience. This type of content encourages interaction and helps build a community around your profile.

Action Tip: Aim to post at least once a day, even if every video isn't "viral-worthy." Consistency helps build visibility over time, and each post is an opportunity to reach a new audience.

Strategy Insight: Consistent posting not only helps you stay visible but also allows you to experiment and find what content resonates most with your audience. Over time, this iterative process can lead to stronger engagement and increase your chances of hitting viral success.

Using Consistent Thumbnails

Thumbnails are the first impression your videos make, and using consistent styles can make your profile look polished and cohesive. When viewers visit your profile, a well-organized and visually appealing layout can encourage them to explore more of your content and follow your account.

Unified Style

Choose a consistent font, text size, and colour scheme for your thumbnails. This makes it easier for viewers to understand what each video is about briefly and gives your profile a professional look.

Brand Recognition

Using the same style for your thumbnails helps establish your brand identity. When viewers see your distinctive thumbnails in their feed, they'll immediately recognize your content.

Highlight Key Points

Use your thumbnails to highlight what the video is about. Keep the text short and impactful, and ensure it stands out against the background image.

Making Your Profile Appealing

Your profile is often the first place new viewers go to learn more about you. A well-organized, visually consistent profile can turn casual viewers into followers.

Cohesive Look

Avoid using random styles, fonts, and colours for your thumbnails. This can make your profile look scattered and unorganized. Instead, stick to a consistent theme to make your profile look neat and inviting.

Easy Navigation

Consistent thumbnails help viewers quickly identify the content they're interested in. This can increase their likelihood of engaging with your videos and ultimately following your account.

Action Tip: Use a consistent design for your video thumbnails, including text font, size, and colours. This not only makes your profile look professional but also helps potential followers quickly understand what your content is about.

Strategy Insight: A cohesive profile layout with consistent thumbnails can enhance your brand image, making it easier for viewers to recognize and connect with your content. This visual consistency, combined with regular posting, increases the chances of turning profile visitors into loyal followers.

Content Creation Boosters

Create a Posting Calendar
Develop a content calendar for the next two weeks. Plan out at least one post per day, even if it's something simple like a quick reaction video or an update. Focus on consistency over complexity. How does having a clear schedule improve your workflow?

Batch Record Multiple Videos in One Session
Set aside time to film multiple TikTok videos in one session. Choose a few topics that are trending or relevant to your niche and focus on getting them all done in one go. This way, you'll have content ready to post for the week. How does batching content affect your ability to stay consistent?

Analyse Your Posting Frequency
Review your current posting habits. Are you posting regularly, or are there gaps between uploads? Create a challenge for yourself to post daily for the next 7 days. Afterward, analyse how this consistency affects your engagement and follower growth.

Recycle and Repurpose Content
Take one of your older videos that performed well and repurpose it with a new angle or updated information. You don't always need to reinvent the wheel just tweak a successful format or idea. How can you make small changes to refresh old content?

ACTION 6
ENGAGE THROUGH
COMMENTS
& COMMUNITY

What You Will Learn

• RESPOND TO COMMENTS • LEVERAGE FEEDBACK •
• CREATE VIDEO RESPONSES • SPARK CONVERSATIONS •
• BUILD A SUPPORTIVE COMMUNITY •

Action 6 –
Engage with Comments and Community

Engagement is key to building a loyal following on TikTok and increasing the reach of your videos. When your content sparks a conversation, it shows the algorithm that your video is engaging and worth promoting to a broader audience. Actively engaging with your viewers in the comments section can significantly boost your visibility and help foster a sense of community around your content.

Why Engagement Matters

TikTok's algorithm places a high value on engagement. Videos that generate comments, likes, and shares signal to the platform that the content is resonating with viewers. This increased interaction not only boosts the video's visibility but also enhances your profile's credibility as an active and responsive creator.

What You Need to Do

Increase Video Reach: The more interaction your video receives, the more likely TikTok is to promote it on the "For You" page, as the algorithm interprets high engagement as a sign of quality content.

Build Community: Actively engaging with your viewers in the comments section helps create a community around your content. When followers feel acknowledged and valued, they are more likely to continue engaging with your future posts.

Strategies for Effective Engagement

To maximize the impact of your engagement, it's important to respond thoughtfully and creatively to comments. Consider using a variety of methods to interact with your audience:

What You Need to Do

Reply to Comments: Answer questions, thank viewers for their feedback, and participate in ongoing conversations. Your responses can encourage more viewers to comment, creating a lively discussion.

Create Video Responses: For comments that ask interesting questions or provide unique perspectives, consider creating a video response. This not only acknowledges the commenter but also generates new content and keeps the engagement cycle going.

Encourage Interaction: Use call-to-actions (CTAs) in your videos and captions to prompt viewers to comment. Ask for their opinions, experiences, or suggestions, and make it clear that you'll be engaging with their responses.

Strategy insight: A creator posted a video immediately after a major event, and viewers commented on how quickly it was made. The creator responded to these comments with a follow-up video explaining their process, which not only engaged the initial commenters but also drew in new viewers who were curious about the content creation process.

Creating a Positive Community

Creating a positive and supportive community around your content is essential for sustained engagement and building a loyal following on TikTok. A thriving community not only boosts your visibility but also fosters a sense of connection and trust between you and your audience. This foundation of trust and support can significantly enhance your long-term success on the platform.

Establishing a Welcoming Environment: The tone you set in your comment section and videos will define the atmosphere of your community. Be mindful of how you interact with viewers and encourage positive behaviour among your followers.

Lead by Example: Respond to comments with kindness, empathy, and enthusiasm. Show appreciation for positive feedback and handle criticism constructively. Your approach to communication sets the standard for how viewers should interact within your community.

Encourage Respectful Dialogue: Explicitly ask your followers to be respectful and considerate in their interactions with you and each other. If your content addresses sensitive or controversial topics, remind viewers to share their thoughts respectfully.

Engage Regularly and Authentically

Consistent and genuine engagement helps deepen the connection between you and your followers. When viewers feel that their opinions are valued, they are more likely to continue engaging with your content.

Respond to Comments Thoughtfully: Take the time to reply to comments in a meaningful way, especially those that ask questions or share personal experiences. A thoughtful response shows that you care about your viewers' input.

Highlight Community Contributions: Feature comments or ideas from your followers in your videos. This could involve creating content based on their suggestions or doing shout-outs to loyal fans. This not only acknowledges their contributions but also motivates others to participate.

Content That Appeals with Your Audience

Understand your audience's interests and preferences to create content that aligns with their values and needs. When your content resonates on a personal level, it strengthens the bond between you and your community.

Address Common Questions: Identify issues or questions that your audience often faces and create content that provides solutions or insights. This shows that you are attentive to their needs and willing to offer valuable support.

Encourage Sharing of Personal Stories: Use your content to encourage viewers to share their experiences related to your videos. This can create a space where followers connect with each other, building a sense of shared experience and community.

Handle Negative Comments with Grace

No matter how positive your community is, you may occasionally encounter negativity. How you handle these situations can impact your community's perception and morale.

Respond Calmly or Ignore: If a negative comment is constructive, respond calmly and acknowledge the feedback. For malicious comments, consider ignoring or deleting them to prevent toxic interactions from taking root.

Set Clear Boundaries: Establish clear rules for what kind of behaviour is acceptable in your community. This can be communicated in your bio, pinned comments, or directly in your videos. Make it clear that harassment or disrespect will not be tolerated.

Foster Connections Among Followers

Encourage interactions between your followers to create a network of support within your community. This can help turn casual viewers into dedicated followers and advocates of your content.

Host Q&A Sessions or Live Streams: Use TikTok's live features to interact with your audience in real-time. Answer their questions, discuss relevant topics, and let them share their thoughts and experiences with each other.

Create Challenges or Collaborative Content: Invite your community to participate in challenges or create content using a specific hashtag. This not only increases engagement but also strengthens the sense of belonging and collaboration among your followers.

Action Tip: Regularly show appreciation for your followers by acknowledging their support and contributions. Small gestures, like liking their comments or featuring them in your content, can go a long way in building loyalty and trust.

Strategy Insight: A positive and engaged community can become your greatest asset on TikTok. Not only does it boost your visibility and reach, but it also creates a supportive environment that sustains long-term growth and success.

Content Creation Boosters

Respond to 5 Comments on Your Latest Video
Take the time to engage with your audience by responding to at least five comments on your latest video. Be thoughtful in your replies, asking follow-up questions or adding value to the conversation. How does this interaction boost your engagement and viewer loyalty

Create a Video Reply to a Comment
Find an interesting or frequently asked question in the comments section of one of your videos. Use TikTok's "reply with a video" feature to create a direct response. How does turning a comment into content help build community?

Ask a Question in Your Next Post
In your next video, include a direct question for your viewers to answer in the comments. It could be something relevant to the video's topic or a fun, engaging prompt. How does this encourage conversation and boost interaction?

Pin a Comment to Spark a Discussion
Pin a thoughtful or intriguing comment on one of your videos to encourage more people to join the discussion. Pay attention to how this affects the flow of comments and viewer engagement.

Create a Poll Clip or Interactive Post
Post a video that includes a poll or invites viewers to share their opinion on a trending topic. Encourage them to comment on their choice and engage with their responses. How does adding an interactive element change the engagement?

ACTION 7
TAP INTO
TRENDING
TOPICS

What You Will Learn

- STAY UP-TO-DATE ON TRENDS •
- ACT QUICKLY •
- CREATE CONTENT AROUND POPULAR THEMES •
- TRENDING SOUNDS AND HASHTAGS •
- ADD YOUR UNIQUE SPIN •

Action 7
Tap into Trending Topics

Creating content that aligns with trending topics can significantly increase your chances of going viral on TikTok. Whether it's a new product release, breaking news, a viral meme, or a hot celebrity moment, using these topics allows you to tap into existing conversations and capture the attention of a wider and global audience. Staying current and reacting quickly to trends helps you capitalize on heightened interest, boosting your video's discoverability and engagement. And this is exactly what you want!

Why Trending Topics Matter

People are naturally drawn to content that is relevant and timely. By aligning your videos with what's currently popular, you increase the likelihood of your content being discovered and shared. TikTok's algorithm favours content that reflects trending topics, as it aims to keep users engaged with fresh and relevant material.

Increased Discoverability: Trending topics often come with popular hashtags and high search volumes, making your content easier to find. Being part of these conversations increases your chances of appearing on the "For You" page.

Higher Engagement Potential: Videos about trending subjects are more likely to be shared, commented on, and liked, as they resonate with what viewers are already interested in.

Identifying and Acting on Trends

To capitalize on current trends, it's essential to stay informed and be ready to create content as soon as news breaks. While being well prepared, a content creator can stay ahead of the game by swiftly posting videos as soon as official releases, such as those from Apple or Tesla, are announced. By capitalizing on the heightened interest and search activity surrounding these events, they can maximize views and engagement. This proactive approach aligns their content perfectly with trending topics, resulting in a significant spike in visibility and audience interaction.

Follow Reliable Sources: Keep up with tech and entertainment news by following trusted websites, influencers, and social media accounts. Use tools like Google Trends and Twitter's trending section to see what people are talking about in real-time.

Prepare in Advance: For recurring events, like major tech product launches or annual awards shows, prepare scripts and ideas in advance. This way, you can post content immediately when the news hits.

Be Ready to Pivot: If a surprising news story or viral moment occurs, be prepared to pivot your content strategy. Posting timely reactions or takes on unexpected events can boost your visibility.

Finding Your Content Creation Niche

When it comes to TikTok success, one of the most crucial steps is identifying your niche. A niche is the specific content area or topic you focus on, which allows you to build a dedicated audience. But more than just a strategy, your niche should reflect something you're genuinely passionate about. Creating content around topics that excite you will make your TikTok journey more enjoyable and sustainable.

Why Finding the Right Niche Matters

You need to be able to work as natural as possible with these areas, authenticity, consistency and community. Content should reflect your real interests and personality then it will resonate more with the viewers. Audiences can tell when you're genuinely invested in what you're sharing. Sticking to a niche makes it easier to create consistent content. It helps you focus your energy and build a reliable content schedule. A niche helps you build a loyal community of followers who share similar interests. These followers are more likely to engage with your content, share it, and become long-term supporters.

Let Popular Topics Inspire You

While finding a niche that aligns with your personal interests is key, you can always draw inspiration from trending topics to give your content a creative twist. If you're unsure where to start, or you're looking to keep things fresh, here are some of TikTok's most popular content areas that can serve as a creative spin doctor for your own videos:

Tech Reviews

Share your thoughts on the latest gadgets and whether they're worth the hype. For example, create a comparison video of two popular smartphones or give a hands-on review of a trending tech gadget like a new smartwatch or gaming console.

Reactions

Post real-time reactions to movie trailers, music video releases, or celebrity news. For instance, share your thoughts on a newly released film trailer or react to a viral award show moment. You could also join in discussions around popular TV shows or recent celebrity trends.

Fitness Challenges

Try out a trending fitness routine and share your progress and results. Participate in viral fitness challenges like "30 Days of Yoga" or document your journey with popular fitness apps. You can also recreate famous workout routines from athletes or influencers.

DIY Tutorials

Teach your audience a simple DIY project related to current trends, like home decor, fashion hacks, or even beauty tips. For example, you could demonstrate how to make custom clothing, create viral home organization tips, or share simple skincare routines.

Personal Experiences

Share your take on trending lifestyle changes, such as remote work tips, balancing mental wellness, or productivity hacks. You could document your work-from-home routine or share personal development stories, like how you overcame delaying your daily tasks or built a morning routine.

Food Trends
Join in on popular food-related TikTok trends by recreating viral recipes or sharing cooking hacks. For example, try the latest TikTok food craze (like "pasta chips" or "cloud bread") and post your own take on it. You can also offer easy, step-by-step recipe tutorials for quick and trending meals.

Travel and Adventure
Post your travel experiences and hidden gem locations. Even if you aren't currently traveling, you can create "virtual travel" content by showcasing local spots or sharing past trips and adventures. Try vlogging a day in your city or reacting to viral travel destinations.

Skincare and Beauty Tips
Hop on skincare trends by offering tutorials, routines, or reviews of popular beauty products. For example, show your morning or night skincare routine, review trending products like jade rollers, or recreate viral makeup looks.

Educational or How-To Content
Create informative, bite-sized lessons on topics like language learning, tech tutorials, or life hacks. For example, teach your viewers how to use editing software, master TikTok features, or explain simple concepts in areas like finance, photography, or personal growth.

Comedy Skits and Relatable Content
Use humour and relatability to create skits around everyday situations. For instance, poke fun at common workplace struggles, family dynamics, or awkward social interactions. Many creators find viral success through relatable, everyday scenarios turned into short, funny clips.

Unboxing Videos
Film yourself unboxing the latest tech, fashion, or subscription box products. Unboxing videos are highly popular, especially when tied

to major product launches or niche hobbies like gaming, beauty, or collectibles.

Motivational and Inspirational Content

Share personal growth stories or daily affirmations to inspire your audience. You could post motivational content like "a day in the life" routines that emphasize productivity or overcoming challenges.

Fashion

Showcase your latest fashion finds or review popular fashion trends. For example, post a "clothing haul" after a shopping spree from Temu, or give styling tips on how to wear trending fashion pieces.

Content Creation Boosters

Use the Discovery Page

Use TikTok's "Discover" page or tools like TrendTok or Google Trends to identify hashtags and sounds gaining momentum. Pick a trending topic relevant to your niche and brainstorm how you can create a video that adds your unique perspective or twist.

Prepare Content in Advance for Expected Trends

Look ahead at scheduled events or upcoming product launches in your niche, such as award shows, product releases, or big industry conferences. Create videos or scripts ahead of time, so you can post quickly when the trend breaks. How can you be the first to react or share your thoughts on these topics?

Use a Celebrity References in Your Niche

Take a trending celebrity event and relate it to your niche. For example, if your niche is fitness, you could create content around a celebrity's workout routine or react to a viral meme about healthy living. How does this strategy help your content stand out in your field?

Unexpected but Relevant Trends

Sometimes trends from unrelated niches can work well for your content. Explore how you can adapt a trending topic that might seem unrelated but can be used differently for your audience. For instance, if a beauty trend is going viral, how could you tie it into a business or lifestyle niche creatively?

ACTION 8
USE BOLD &
CLEAR
HOOKS

What You Will Learn

- GRAB ATTENTION IN THE FIRST 3 SECONDS -
- KEEP IT SIMPLE -
- TEASE A PAYOFF • VISUAL SHOCK -
- RELATABLE SCENARIOS -

Action 8 -
Use Bold and Clear Hooks

A powerful hook is essential for grabbing attention on TikTok. With users scrolling through an endless stream of videos, your content needs to stand out immediately. A strong, clear hook in the first 2-3 seconds can make viewers stop and watch instead of swiping past. Whether it's a bold statement, a surprising visual, or an intriguing question, the hook sets the tone for your video and entices viewers to stay engaged.

Why Hooks Are Crucial

The hook is the first impression your video makes, and it's your best opportunity to capture attention in a crowded feed. TikTok's algorithm prioritizes videos that keep viewers watching until the end, so a compelling hook can significantly impact your video's performance.

Stop the Scroll: A clear and bold hook catches the viewer's eye and stops them from scrolling past. It could be a humorous claim, a shocking fact, or a visually captivating scene.

Set Expectations: The hook should clearly communicate what the video is about or tease an outcome that viewers will want to see. This keeps them curious and invested in watching more.

Creating Effective Hooks

An effective hook should be immediate, engaging, and relevant to the content of your video. A creator begins a video with, "I can't believe this actually worked!" while showing a dramatic before-and-after result. The combination of a bold statement and a visual hook catches the viewers immediately. Here are some strategies for creating hooks that stand out:

Use Bold Statements: Start with a surprising fact, a controversial statement, or a bold claim that piques curiosity. For example, "This trick can save you hundreds on your next vacation!" immediately grabs attention.

Incorporate Visual Surprises: Show something unexpected in the first frame, such as an unusual location, a funny action, or a sudden transformation. Visual surprises create curiosity and make viewers want to see what happens next.

Ask Intriguing Questions: Pose a question that sparks curiosity or invites viewers to reflect on their own experiences. For example, "Ever wondered why some videos go viral while others don't?" makes viewers want to know the answer.

Types of Hooks to Consider

Hooks are the gateway to keeping your audience engaged on TikTok, and the type of hook you use can make all the difference. There are several styles of hooks that work effectively, each tailored to different types of content and viewer expectations. By using the right kind of hook, you can create videos that immediately capture attention and compel viewers to watch until the very end.

The Visual Hook: Capture attention with striking visuals, such as a unique setup, bright colours, or an unusual scene. For example, starting a video with a colourful explosion of paint or a slow-motion shot can intrigue viewers.

The Tease Hook: Tease an unexpected reveal or outcome. Phrases like "Wait until you see what happens next!" or "You won't believe how this ends!" encourage viewers to stay.

The Challenge Hook: Introduce a challenge or a problem that your video will solve. For instance, "Here's how I fixed my productivity in 30 days" sets up the video as a solution to a common issue.

The Shock Hook: Use an unexpected or shocking statement to grab attention. Something like, "I spent $1,000 on this product and here's what happened" makes viewers curious about the story behind it.

Action Tip: Focus on creating hooks that are bold, clear, and directly related to the main content of your video. Test different types of hooks to see which ones resonate best with your audience and result in higher engagement.

Strategy Insight: A strong hook is the gateway to your video's success. The first few seconds determine whether viewers will engage or scroll past, so invest time in crafting hooks that capture attention and set up your video for maximum impact.

Content Creation Boosters

Test Different Types of Hooks
Create three different video intros using various types of hooks. Post them over a few days and analyse which hook gets the most engagement. What type of hook best captures your audience's attention?

Open with an Unexpected Fact or Statement
Start your next video with a surprising fact or an unexpected statement related to your niche. Reflect on how adding an element of surprise to your hooks affects viewer retention.

Use Visual Cues to Enhance Your Hook
Pair a strong visual cue with your hook, such as a prop, dynamic movement, or a sudden shift in scenery. This visual intrigue should complement your verbal hook to further engage viewers.

Experiment with Tease Hooks
In your next video, use a tease hook that hints at an exciting or unexpected reveal. Phrases like "Wait until you see what happens next!" or "You won't believe how this ends!" encourage viewers to stay until the end. Monitor how this strategy impacts watch time.

Analyse Successful Hooks
Spend some time analysing videos from top creators in your niche. What kinds of hooks are they using in their most viral content? Try recreating a similar hook in your own style to see how it does effect your video's reach?

ACTION 9
SUPRISE
AND TWIST
THE REALITY

What You Will Learn

- TWIST THE EXPECTED •
- CREATE SPIN-OFFS • USE EXAGGERATION •
- BREAK STEREOTYPES • CREATE PERSONAS •

Action 9 –
Play with Expectations
and Twist Reality

One of the most captivating aspects of TikTok is its ability to blur the lines between reality and fiction. Content that twists expectations or bends reality in creative ways often captures attention and encourages viewers to engage, share, and discuss. Whether it's through exaggerated characters, unexpected plot twists, or immersive "method acting," playing with what viewers expect can lead to highly shareable and memorable videos.

Why Twisting Reality Works

Playing with expectations taps into the element of surprise, a powerful tool for grabbing attention and making content stand out. When viewers encounter something that defies their assumptions or portrays reality in an exaggerated way, they are more likely to stop, watch, and share the content with others. This type of content provokes curiosity and often leaves viewers wondering, "Is this real?"

Element of Surprise: Content that challenges norms or expectations can be highly engaging because it subverts what viewers anticipate. This creates a memorable experience and compels them to share the video with others to spark discussions.

Creates Buzz and Conversation: Videos that twist reality or play with personas often go viral because they generate debate and curiosity. People love to speculate about whether the content is genuine or part of a performance, which leads to more comments and shares.

Creating Engaging Characters and Scenarios

One effective way to twist reality is by creating characters or scenarios that are exaggerated versions of real-life roles. A creator pretended to be a ultra-wealthy tech founder, complete with designer clothes and luxury cars. By playing on stereotypes about tech entrepreneurs and exaggerating the "rich kid" persona, they attracted attention and sparked discussions about whether the character was real or just a clever act. This approach leverages recognizable archetypes but with a twist that makes the content unique and compelling.

Invent Exaggerated Personas: Craft characters that are heightened versions of common stereotypes, like the "over-the-top rich kid" or the "comically clueless boss." These personas are relatable yet absurd, making them both engaging and shareable.

Method Acting and Immersion: Fully commit to your character or scenario, staying in role throughout your videos. This level of commitment blurs the line between fiction and reality, making your content more immersive and intriguing.

Playing with Expectations in Storytelling

In TikTok, playing with expectations is a powerful way to keep your audience engaged and surprised. By setting up familiar situations and then introducing unexpected twists or humorous shifts, you can capture viewers' attention and make your content more memorable. Whether you're turning a routine tutorial into something absurd or acting out imaginative scenarios, these sudden shifts in storytelling spark curiosity and laughter, encouraging shares and comments.

The following techniques, such as fake tutorials, pretend scenarios, and clever twists, offer a fun way to keep your content fresh and exciting, ensuring that your audience stays hooked.

The Sudden Twist: Start with a familiar setup but introduce an unexpected twist midway through the video. For example, a video that begins as a standard cooking tutorial might suddenly reveal that the recipe is for something unconventional or humorous, like "how to cook with no ingredients."

Pretend Scenarios: Act out a scenario that's believable but slightly offbeat, such as pretending to work in an imaginary office or acting as a fictional "influencer trainer." These pretend scenarios play with viewers' expectations and add a layer of humour and creativity.

Fake Tutorials and Life Hacks: Create fake tutorials that start like a legitimate how-to video but take an absurd turn. For example, a creator made a video titled "How to Make an Office Chair for $10," but the tutorial turned into a series of overly complicated and humorous steps using random household items, ending with a bizarre "chair" creation. The unexpected turn made the video highly shareable and memorable making viewers laugh and share it for the humour.

Using Humour and Irony

Humour is an essential element in content that twists reality. Exaggeration and irony make your videos entertaining while delivering a subtle commentary on real-world situations.

Exaggerate Real-Life Scenarios: Take a common situation, like a Zoom meeting or a job interview, and amplify the absurdities. This could mean portraying a meeting with hilariously unrealistic expectations or a job interview with bizarre requirements.

Use Satire: Poke fun at popular trends or societal norms by presenting them in a ridiculous or exaggerated way. This can resonate with viewers who recognize the underlying truth in your humour.

Action Tip: Experiment with creating exaggerated characters or scenarios that challenge expectations. Fully commit to your roles and use humour to make your content engaging and memorable.

Strategy Insight: Content that twists reality or plays with viewers' expectations stands out because it offers a fresh perspective on familiar themes. By surprising your audience and keeping them guessing, you increase the likelihood of your videos being shared and discussed, boosting your reach and engagement.

Content Creation Boosters

Start with Normal and End with a Twist
Take a standard format like a tutorial or daily routine video and surprise your audience with an unexpected twist halfway through. How does your audience react when you break away from their expectations?

Create a Character with an Unusual Storyline
Develop a recurring character who lives in an exaggerated or fictional reality. Think of a quirky profession or a scenario that isn't quite normal. How does this persona let you play with reality and surprise viewers?

Mix Serious with Absurd
In your next video, start with a serious topic but slowly introduce absurd elements that catch viewers off-guard. How do viewers respond to the mix of tones?

Recreate an Everyday Scenario with a Twist
Think of a common activity like cooking, cleaning, or commuting and give it an unexpected twist. Perhaps you "cook" using only office supplies or clean a room with bizarre tools. How does exaggerating or flipping expectations lead to more shares and engagement?

ACTION 10
WHEN VIRAL
RIDE ON THE
MOMENTUM

What You Will Learn

• MAXIMIZE THE VIRAL MOMENTUM •
• CREATE SPIN-OFFS • ANALYZE VIRAL SUCCESS •
• ENGAGE WITH NEW FOLLOWERS •
• RIDE THE TREND WAVE •

Action 10 –
Ride on the Momentum

When one of your TikTok videos goes viral, it's a golden opportunity to maximize your reach and grow your following. Capitalizing on viral success means more than just enjoying the initial spike in views, it's about strategically creating new content that builds on the excitement and attention your video has generated. By spinning off new ideas from the viral clip and adding unique twists, you can keep your audience engaged and expand your visibility even further.

Why Riding the Momentum is Crucial

Viral moments on TikTok are often short-lived and if you don't act quickly, the surge in interest can dissipate just as fast as it arrived. Leveraging the momentum of a viral video helps you maintain high engagement levels and solidify your connection with new followers.

Sustain and Grow Your Audience: Following up on a viral hit with related content helps keep new viewers interested and encourages them to become long-term followers. The initial interest is a perfect time to showcase more of what you offer.

Maximize Engagement and Reach: The TikTok algorithm favours accounts that post consistently and engage actively. By building on your viral video, you can continue to receive algorithmic boosts that increase your content's visibility.

Creating Spin-Offs from Viral Clips

Once you have a viral video, it's time to think creatively about how to expand on the theme or topic of the original content. Building off a successful video can help keep the momentum going, attract new viewers and strengthen your connection with your existing audience. Here are some detailed strategies for generating new content ideas:

Build on the Same Theme with a Twist: When your viral video centers around a specific theme, consider exploring different angles or aspects of that theme. This approach allows you to maintain continuity while offering fresh content that keeps your audience engaged.

Deep Dive into the Topic: If your viral video was a humorous take on a common frustration, like dealing with work-from-home challenges, create follow-up videos that dive deeper into related scenarios. For instance, you could explore the quirks of different types of colleagues in a virtual meeting or the evolution of your work-from-home setup over time.

Introduce New Perspectives: If your viral video featured a particular character or persona, try presenting the same scenario from another character's viewpoint. This not only keeps the theme familiar but also adds depth and variety, making your content more interesting.

Connect with Current Trends: Incorporate current TikTok trends into your spin-offs. Use trending sounds, challenges, or popular hashtags to tie your new content to what's currently hot on the platform while staying true to your original theme.

Expand the Story or Concept

If your viral video had a narrative or storyline, continuing it with sequels, prequels or parallel stories can keep your audience invested in the ongoing narrative. A creator whose video about a comical office situation went viral followed up with videos introducing the "new boss" character and their humorous interactions with the team. Each episode added a new dynamic to the storyline, keeping viewers hooked.

Sequels and Prequels: Develop a series that follows the characters or storyline established in the viral video. If your video was about a comedic incident in the office, create sequels showing what happens next or prequels that explore how the situation unfolded.

Introduce New Characters or Plot Twists: Adding new characters or unexpected developments can keep your content fresh. For example, introduce a rival to your original character, or reveal a surprising backstory that changes the context of the original video.

Create a Mini-Series: Turn your viral video into a mini-series by developing episodes around different aspects of the story. This approach encourages viewers to follow along and look forward to the next clip increasing the engagement.

Branch Out with Related Formats

Expand the scope of your viral content by experimenting with different formats that still relate to the original video. This approach keeps your content fresh and engaging without straying too far from what initially attracted your audience.

Behind-the-Scenes Content: Share insights into how you created your viral video. This could include creative processes or technical tips. Behind-the-scenes content not only deepens your audience's connection but also provides valuable information for aspiring creators.

Tutorials and "How-To" Videos: If your viral content included a specific skill, process or challenge create tutorials that teach your audience how to replicate it. For example, if your video featured a unique editing technique, break down the steps in a tutorial.

Collaborations: Encourage your followers to create their own versions of your viral content using duets, stitches or challenges. Highlight the best ones in a compilation video or collaborate with other creators to bring fresh perspectives to your content. A creator who gained attention with a viral video about "weird things I learned living abroad" followed up with "how-to" videos on navigating cultural differences, collaborating with other creators to discuss their unique experiences.

Integrate Followers Requests

Use the momentum from your viral hit to engage with your audience and generate ideas for new content. Your followers can be a rich source of inspiration for new content. Pay attention to their comments, suggestions and questions to identify topics they are curious about or aspects of your viral video they want to see explored further.

Respond to Comments: Create videos that directly address common questions or requests from your audience. This not only provides valuable content but also shows that you value and engage with your community and keeps the viral video fresh in people's minds as they continue to interact with it.

Incorporate Fan Ideas: If viewers start speculating or creating theories around your viral video, consider incorporating these ideas into your follow-up content. Acknowledging and playing off fan interpretations can deepen their connection to your content.

A creator whose video about a fictional universe went viral noticed fans theorizing about certain characters' backstories. They created a series of follow-up videos exploring these theories, validating and engaging their community in the process.

Content Creation Boosters

Post a Follow-Up or Sequel

Once your video goes viral, immediately follow up with a sequel or continuation. For example, if your original video featured a challenge or skit, create a "Part 2" or a behind-the-scenes look at how you made the viral video. How does continuing the conversation help keep your audience engaged?

Engage with Your Audience Directly

After a viral hit, interact with the new followers and commenters by asking questions or responding to popular comments. Post a video addressing fan reactions or answering questions that arose from the viral video. How does this direct interaction strengthen your connection with viewers?

Create Reaction Videos

Use your viral video as a springboard for reaction content. For example, create a video reacting to your audience's comments, or do a commentary on what surprised you about the video's success. How does responding to the buzz around your viral moment build community?

Reuse the Viral Video

Repurpose your viral video for other platforms or formats. You could create a shorter version, highlight specific elements in a new way, or adapt it for Instagram, YouTube, or other social media platforms. How does sharing the viral content in different ways extend its life and reach?

COMMENTS
ENGAGEMENT MATTERS MORE THAN LIKES

What You Will Learn

- ENGAGEMENT SIGNALS TO THE ALGORITHM •
- COMMENTS FOSTER COMMUNITY •
- COMMENTS DRIVE EXTENDED WATCH TIME •
- CONVERSATIONS INCREASES SHARES •

The Power of Comments

Why Engagement Matters

While likes are often viewed as a key indicator of success, comments hold a much higher value on TikTok. They signify deeper engagement and interaction, which the algorithm rewards by boosting the video's visibility. When a video generates a lot of comments and replies, TikTok sees this as a signal that the content is highly engaging, increasing its chances of being shown to more users on the "For You" page.

Therefor its important to create content that encourages viewers to comment and interact with each other. This not only enhances visibility but also fosters a community around your content. TikTok aims to keep users engaged on the platform. Videos that spark discussions and generate a "buzz" in the comment section are more likely to go viral, as they fulfill this goal.

Comments Matter More Than Likes

Deeper Engagement: A like is a quick tap, but a comment requires more thought and effort. When users take the time to comment, it shows that they are genuinely interested in the content and want to engage with it on a deeper level.

Spark Conversations: Comments often lead to discussions. When viewers start replying to each other, it creates long threads of conversation, which signals to TikTok that the content is highly engaging and encourages people to spend more time on the platform. Once you posted a clip comment it your self with questions that can spark the conversations.

Boost Visibility: The TikTok algorithm favours videos that generate a high level of interaction. Videos with active comment sections are more likely to be pushed to more viewers because they keep users engaged and on the app longer.

Community Building: Comments help build a community around your content. When users see an active comment section, they are more likely to join the conversation, increasing the video's reach and engagement.

How to Encourage More Comments

Ask Open-Ended Questions: Pose questions in your video or caption that invite viewers to share their thoughts, opinions, or experiences. For example, "What do you think will happen next?" or "Have you ever experienced this?"

Create Controversial or Debatable Content: Content that sparks debate or controversy can drive a high volume of comments. Be careful to remain respectful and thoughtful in your approach to avoid negative backlash.

Respond to Comments: Engaging with your audience by responding to their comments encourages further discussion. Join the discussion with you point of view to keep it alive and trigger the algorithm happy. A simple "Thanks for sharing your thoughts!" or "That's a great point!" can keep the conversation going.

Use Call-to-Actions (CTAs): Directly ask your viewers to comment on specific aspects of your video. For instance, "Comment below if you agree!" or "Let me know your thoughts on this in the comments!"

Highlight Viewer Comments in Future Videos: Mention or show screenshots of interesting comments in your next video. This makes viewers feel valued and more likely to comment again, hoping to be featured. This is mainly for community building as mentioning people doesn't increase the likeliness to get more views.

Make the First Two Comments Yourself: As soon as you post a video, make the first two comments yourself so people have something to interact with. It's like an icebreaker at a party someone needs to start the conversation, and often no one wants to go first.

Creation Boosters

Reply to Comments with Video Responses
Use TikTok's feature to reply to comments with a video. Choose a comment that had a lot of engagement or asks an interesting question and turn it into a new piece of content by reply with a video.

Ask a Specific Question in Your Next Post
Create a video that ends with a direct question for your audience. Whether it's asking for their opinion or a fun question. How does asking for feedback increase the volume and quality of comments on your video?

Use Comments to Spark New Content Ideas
Scroll through comments on your most popular videos and identify recurring themes or questions. Use these comments as inspiration for your next video or series. How does using viewer feedback help you stay in tune with your audience?

Start a Conversation Around a Hot Topic
Post a video addressing a trending or controversial topic and encourage viewers to share their opinions in the comments. Make sure to engage with as many responses as possible to keep the conversation alive.

Turn Positive Comments into Testimonials
If you receive positive feedback or compliments in the comments, highlight them in your future videos. Create a video showing some of the best comments or thanking your audience for their input.

VIRAL EDITS
TOOLS TO
BOOST YOUR
TIKTOK CLIPS

What You Will Learn

• MASTER QUICK CUTS • USE TRENDING SOUNDS •
• CREATE VISUAL CONSISTENCY •
• SUBTITLES FOR CLARITY & ENGAGEMENT •
• OPTIMIZE FOR MOBILE VIEWING •

Viral Edits

Edit Your Clips Like a Pro

Creating a viral TikTok video isn't just about what you film it's also about how you present it. Effective video editing can be the difference between a clip that catches fire and one that fizzles out. Lets explore key editing strategies and online tools that can help you craft videos that captivate viewers from the first second to the last.

Capturing Attention from the Start

The first few seconds of your video are critical. This is your chance to grab the viewer's attention and make them want to keep watching. A strong hook should be both visual and audible, clearly stating what the clip is about and what viewers will gain from watching it.

Visual Hook: Use eye-catching visuals right from the start. This could be a surprising scene, a quick movement, or an unexpected action.

Audible Hook: Use a bold statement or question in the first second to make viewers curious. For example, start with phrases like "Did you know...?" or "Watch this if you want to...".

Action Tip: Combine the visual and audible hooks to create a powerful opening that immediately engages viewers. For example, if you're demonstrating a quick recipe, start with a close-up shot of the finished dish while saying, "This is the easiest dessert you'll ever make!"

Strategy Insight: The TikTok algorithm prioritizes videos that keep viewers engaged from the very beginning. A strong hook not only captures attention but also boosts the chances of your video being featured on the "For You" page.

Fast Clips and Keep the Pace Up

TikTok thrives on short, snappy content. If your video lingers too long on a scene or explanation, viewers will lose interest and swipe away. To maintain a fast pace:

Narrow it down: If you have two lines of dialogue or explanation, try to condense them into one impactful line.

Rapid Cuts: Use quick cuts between scenes to keep the visual energy high. Avoid long pauses or slow transitions.

Visual Variety: Switch between different angles or zoom levels to keep the visual flow dynamic. Even subtle changes can maintain viewer interest.

Action Tip: Review your video and cut out any unnecessary pauses or filler words. Aim for each scene to last no more than 2-3 seconds before switching to a new angle or action.

Strategy Insight: Shorter clips are more likely to be rewatched, increasing your overall watch time a key factor that TikTok considers when deciding which videos to promote.

Making Your Message Clear

Text overlays can enhance your video by reinforcing key points, adding context, or simply making the content more accessible. Tools like CapCut Pro offer advanced text features, including automated subtitles that can highlight specific words as they are spoken.

Automated Subtitles: Use tools like CapCut Pro to generate automatic captions. This is crucial for viewers watching without sound and can increase engagement.

Effective Text Styles: Choose contrasting colours like yellow with black borders to make your text stand out. Avoid using white text with black borders, as it can blend into the background.

Highlighting Key Phrases: Highlight important words or phrases in sync with your voiceover. This guides viewers' attention and emphasizes key points.

Action Tip: Use CapCut Pro's automated caption feature to add subtitles to your videos. Experiment with bold, contrasting colours like yellow with black borders to ensure the text is easy to read on any background.

Strategy Insight: Videos with clear and well-placed text overlays are more likely to hold viewers' attention, especially when they watch without sound. This can lead to longer watch times and more shares.

Voice Over with a Personal Touch

A well-executed voiceover can make your content more relatable and engaging. Use a friendly and enthusiastic tone to guide viewers through the video and highlight key points.

Match the Energy: Your voiceover should match the energy of the content. For fast-paced clips, use a lively tone for more serious topics, a calm and clear delivery works best.

Timing is Everything: Ensure that your voiceover aligns perfectly with the visuals. Mistimed narration can confuse viewers and disrupt the flow of your video.

Action Tip: Record your voiceover in segments to ensure each part is perfectly timed with your visuals. Use tools like InShot or CapCut to edit and sync your voiceover precisely.

Strategy Insight: A voiceover that matches the visuals and energy of the content helps build a stronger connection with viewers, encouraging them to engage with and share your video.

Enhancing Voice Overs with AI: ElevenLabs

Voiceovers can add a professional and engaging touch to your TikTok videos but recording them perfectly can be time-consuming. This is where AI tools like ElevenLabs.io come in. ElevenLabs provides the most natural-sounding AI-generated voices currently available, making it easy to create high-quality voiceovers without the need for a professional recording setup.

Creating Natural-Sounding Narration: ElevenLabs uses advanced AI to produce voices that sound realistic and engaging. This can be especially useful for creators who want to maintain a consistent tone and pace across their videos. When using ElevenLabs or similar AI voice tools, avoid using periods (.) and commas (,) in your text input. This will help create a faster and smoother flow in the voiceover, making the narration sound more conversational and natural.

Action Tip: Use ElevenLabs to generate voiceovers for your TikTok videos. Experiment with different voices and speeds to find the perfect match for your content style. This can save time and ensure that your voiceovers are always clear and professional.

Strategy Insight: High-quality voiceovers can elevate the viewer experience and make your content more accessible. Using AI-generated voices allows for quick adjustments and multiple takes without the hassle of re-recording manually.

Using Trending Music to Increase Your Message

Choosing the right music is essential for enhancing the mood and impact of your TikTok videos. Trending music, especially dramatic or high-energy tracks, can intensify your message and make your content more engaging. TikTok's algorithm often prioritizes videos that use popular sounds, which can increase your chances of being featured on the "For You" page.

Dramatic Music: Use dramatic music to build anticipation or emphasize key moments in your video. This works well for storytelling or surprising reveals, drawing the viewer in and making your content more memorable.

Ambient Music: When your video has silent or less active parts, consider adding ambient music as a subtle background layer. This prevents awkward silences and maintains a consistent flow, making your video feel more polished and professional.

Action Tip: Search TikTok's "Sounds" library for trending tracks that align with your video's theme. Experiment with different genres to see which complements your content best. Remember, music not only enhances the viewing experience but can also influence how the algorithm promotes your video.

Strategy Insight: Using trending music can significantly boost your video's visibility. When paired with effective storytelling or visuals, the right soundtrack can elevate your content and keep viewers engaged throughout the entire clip.

Online Tools for Editing Viral Clips

Here are some must-have tools for editing your TikTok videos and making them stand out.

Using advanced editing tools can set your content apart and make it more visually appealing. This not only helps retain viewers but also increases the likelihood of your videos being shared, ultimately boosting their viral potential.

Familiarize yourself with these tools and use them to experiment with different editing styles. Try combining features from multiple apps to create unique and engaging content.

CapCut Pro: This powerful editing tool offers advanced features like automated subtitles, trending text styles, and a wide range of filters and transitions. It's user-friendly and integrates seamlessly with TikTok.

Website: https://www.capcut.com/

Inshot: A versatile video editor with options for trimming, cutting, and adding music. InShot is excellent for quick edits and adding creative effects to your clips.

Website: https://inshot.com/

Canva: Perfect for creating eye-catching thumbnails, intros, and outros. Canva offers a range of templates and design elements that can enhance the visual appeal of your videos.

Website: https://www.canva.com/

Splice: A robust editing app that allows for precise cuts, advanced transitions, and sound editing. Ideal for creating polished, professional-looking TikTok videos.

Website: https://spliceapp.com/

Veed.io: An online tool that offers automated subtitles, video trimming, and a host of other editing features. It's great for adding professional touches to your content.

Website: https://www.veed.io/

AI SCRIPTS
CRAFTING
ENGAGING
SCRIPTS

What You Will Learn

- DETAILED CONTEXT · SPECIFIC PROMPTS ·
- ITERATIVELY REFINE YOUR SCRIPTS ·
- STRONG CALL-TO-ACTIONS ·
- SCRIPT TIMING TO VISUALS ·

AI Scripts

Crafting Engaging Scripts

Creating a compelling script is the backbone of any successful TikTok video. With tools like ChatGPT, you can quickly generate crisp, engaging and well-structured scripts that capture attention from the first word. AI can help streamline your creative process, offering fresh ideas and refining your content to ensure it resonates with your audience. For shorter TikTok clips, the free version of ChatGPT works perfectly fine and offers more than enough capability to generate quick, effective scripts.

Feeding Context for Better Results

The key to getting the most out of ChatGPT is providing detailed context. The more information you give the AI, the more relevant and tailored the script it generates will be.

Include Background Information: If you're creating a video about a current news topic, include links, relevant data, and key points you want to cover. This ensures the AI understands the nuances of the subject and generates content that is accurate and engaging.

Define Your Audience and Tone: Specify who your audience is by age, occupation or by interest like tech, fashion, sports or food oriented and the tone you want as humorous, serious or inspirational. This helps the AI produce a script that aligns with your brand and message.

When feeding context, use a prompt like, "Generate a 15-second script on the benefits of the new iPhone, targeting tech-savvy millennials with a humorous tone." This level of detail helps ChatGPT produce a script that closely matches your vision.

Iterative Process for Perfecting Your Script

Don't settle for the first draft. Use an iterative approach to refine your script, enhancing its clarity and impact. Start by generating a basic draft, then review it and identify areas that could be more engaging or concise. Ask specific questions to improve it, such as, "Does this opening grab attention?" or "Is the call-to-action clear and effective?" By tweaking and revising, you'll gradually build a script that better aligns with your goals. This process allows you to experiment with tone, pacing, and delivery until the script flows naturally and resonates with your audience. Remember, even small adjustments can lead to significant improvements in how your video is received.

Generate Initial Drafts: Start by generating a basic script. Don't worry if it's not perfect this is just a foundation to build upon. If it's too long or lacks impact you could prompt, "Shorten this script to 10 seconds and add an engaging hook at the start." This way, ChatGPT will produce a tighter, more compelling version.

Request Specific Edits: Review the draft and ask ChatGPT for specific changes, such as "make this section more engaging" or "use more buzz words" This targeted feedback helps refine the script to better suit your needs.

Focus on Flow and Engagement: Ensure the script flows naturally and includes hooks that grab attention. For instance, starting with a question or surprising fact can engage viewers right from the beginning.

Using Specific Prompts

Specific prompts generate more focused and effective scripts. Clearly defining the length, tone, and content focus of your script helps ChatGPT produce better results. As you continue working with the tool, you'll get better at crafting prompts that yield the precise output you need.

Create Short-Form Content: For TikTok, concise scripts are crucial. Use prompts like, "Create a 10-second script introducing a surprising fact about space exploration in an exciting tone."

Define Content Structure: If you want a script with multiple elements, outline this structure. For example, "Write a 15-second script that starts with a hook, introduces a problem, and ends with a call to action."

For trending topics, try prompts like, "Generate a quick, catchy script that summarizes the latest iPhone features in a fun and upbeat manner."

Crafting Call-to-Actions (CTAs)

Strong CTAs encourage viewers to engage with your content, whether it's liking, sharing or commenting. Use AI to craft compelling CTAs that fit naturally within your script.

Include in Script Prompts: When asking ChatGPT for a script, include the CTA in your prompt. For example, "Write a 10-second script about the best productivity apps with a CTA to comment on their favourite app."

Test Different Variations: Experiment with different types of CTAs to see which ones resonate most with your audience. For instance, compare "Follow for more tech tips!" with "Comment your favourite app below!"

Visualizing and Timing Your Script

After crafting your script, visualize how it will play out on screen. This helps you match the pacing and ensure the script fits within TikTok's time constraints.

Time Your Script: Read the script out loud while timing it. This helps you adjust the length and ensures the content fits within TikTok's 15 to 60-second format.

Before using ChatGPT, brainstorm and outline your video. Include the key points you want to cover and the tone you want to convey. Feed this outline into ChatGPT to generate a structured script, then refine it until it meets your needs.

A well-crafted script sets the foundation for your video. By using AI tools like ChatGPT, you can streamline the scripting process, allowing more time for shooting and editing, and ultimately improving the overall quality of your content. Leveraging AI for script refinement not only saves time but also enhances creativity, giving you more bandwidth to focus on delivering engaging, high-quality videos.

Reflections

As you finish this book, remember that success on TikTok isn't just about going viral once it's about understanding what works, being adaptable, and continuously learning from your audience. Each video you create is an opportunity to experiment, engage, and refine your content.

Take a moment to reflect on your own journey and the insights you've gained. How can you apply what you've learned to create meaningful, engaging content that resonates with your audience? Don't be afraid to make mistakes every post is part of the process of finding your unique voice and style on TikTok.

Most importantly, keep pushing your creative boundaries, stay consistent, and have fun with it. Viral success may come unexpectedly, but with the right strategies, dedication and a touch of creativity, you'll be ready when it does. Now, as a final resource, explore the TikTok Glossary to further deepen your understanding of the platform and its language.

TikTok Glossary

To help you navigate the world of TikTok more effectively, I've included a list of key terms and definitions used throughout the platform. If you're new to TikTok then understanding these terms will give you a clearer grasp of the platform and techniques discussed in this book. Use this glossary as a quick reference to familiarize yourself with the language of TikTok.

Term	Definition
For You Page (FYP)	The main feed where TikTok shows curated videos based on user behaviour.
Hashtags (#)	Categories of topics related to clips that make it discoverable on TikTok.
Duet	A feature allowing users to create side-by-side videos with someone else's content.
Stitch	Let's users take a portion of someone else's video and include it in their own.
Likes	Hearts that show viewers enjoyed the video but provide less impact than comments.
Comments	Written feedback or reactions under videos that drive higher engagement.
Shares	Sharing videos with others on TikTok or other platforms, increasing reach.
Challenges	Trends that encourage users to perform a specific task or action, often tied to a hashtag.
TikTok Trends	Popular actions, themes, or sounds widely shared across the platform.
Creator Fund	TikTok's program to pay creators for high-performing videos based on views and engagement.
TikTok Ads	Paid advertisements on TikTok including in-feed videos and branded hashtags.
Profile Views	A metric showing how many users have visited a creator's profile.
Follow/Followers	Users who subscribe to another account's content.
TikTok Analytics	Data on video performance, available to TikTok Pro accounts.
TikTok LIVE	A feature allowing creators with 1000+

	followers to live stream and interact with fans.
Likes to Views Ratio	The percentage of likes in comparison to total video views.
Engagement Rate	A measure of interaction, calculated from likes, comments, and shares versus views.
Bio	The text section on a user's profile where they can describe themselves or their content.
Pinned Videos	Videos that creators can "pin" to the top of their profile for increased visibility.
Filters and Effects	Tools to enhance videos with visuals like colour changes or animated effects.
Creative Tools	Features like transitions, text overlays, and visual effects that enhance videos.
Drafts	Unpublished videos saved to a creator's account for future editing or posting.
Reactions	Videos where users film themselves reacting to another user's content.
POV (Point of View)	A style of video where the creator acts out a scene as if the viewer is a participant.
Lip Syncing	A popular TikTok format where users mouth the words to songs or sound clips.
FYP Optimization	Strategies creators use to get their videos featured on TikTok's "For You Page".
Replays	The number of times viewers rewatch a video, helping boost its reach.
Green Screen	An effect that lets users replace their background with an image or video.
Hashtag Challenge	A branded or user-created challenge promoted by a specific hashtag.
Reaction Video	A type of content where users film their real-time response to another video.

Cross-posting	Sharing the same content on multiple platforms like Instagram, Twitter, etc.
Trending Page	A section in TikTok's Discover area showcasing popular and trending content.
Original Sound	A user-created sound that can be reused by others to make their own videos.
Verified Account	Accounts verified by TikTok, often belonging to public figures, celebrities or brands.
Discovery	The page where users explore new content, trends, and hashtags on TikTok.
Video Reactions	Responses recorded in real time to content, displayed alongside the original.
Duet Chain	A series of Duet videos that continue from one creator to another.
Algorithm	The system TikTok uses to suggest content based on user preferences, views, and interactions.
Viral	Content that quickly spreads and gains large visibility, shares, and engagement.
Looping Videos	Short videos that are designed to loop seamlessly, encouraging replays.
In-feed Ads	Ads that appear in users' video feeds and look like regular TikTok videos.
Voiceover	Adding a recorded narration or commentary to a video.
Muted Videos	Videos where the sound is intentionally turned off, often with text for context.
Trending Hashtags	Popular hashtags that are widely used across TikTok at any given time.
Watch Time	The total amount of time viewers spends watching a video.

Challenges	A video format in which creators perform specific tasks or actions tied to a hashtag or trend.
Video Loops	Videos designed to loop perfectly when they replay, creating seamless transitions.
Watch Time Analysis	Analytics data that reveals how long users watch your videos and when they drop off.
In-App Editing	Editing tools within TikTok used to cut, trim, and add effects to videos before publishing.
Comment Replies	Responses to comments left by viewers, often encouraging engagement and conversation.
Video Thumbnails	The preview image that appears before a video plays, used to entice viewers to watch.
Fan Engagement	The interaction between a creator and their followers, including likes, comments, and shares.
GIFs	Short, looped animations that can be added to videos as visual effects.
Auto-Captions	A TikTok feature that generates subtitles automatically based on spoken content.
AR Filters	Augmented reality effects that add 3D elements to a video, like virtual props or backgrounds.
Collab	When creators work together, either through Duets, Stitches, or in the same video.
Trendjacking	When a creator quickly jumps onto a trending topic or meme to boost visibility.
Storytime Videos	A popular video format where creators narrate interesting or humorous personal stories.
Content Pillars	The main topics or themes a creator focuses on, helping to build a consistent brand.
Behind-the-	Videos showing how content was made,

Scenes (BTS)	offering viewers a look into the creative process.
Niche	A specific topic or area of content that a creator specializes in.
Call to Action (CTA)	A prompt in videos asking viewers to do something, such as like, comment or follow.
Follower Growth	The increase in the number of users who follow a creator over time.
Creator Community	The collective group of creators on TikTok who interact and support each other.
Song Association	A popular video format were creators link songs to certain words or scenarios.
TikTok Algorithm Update	Changes in the algorithm that can affect how videos are promoted or displayed.
In-App Notifications	Alerts and updates within TikTok about new followers, comments, and likes.
Lip Dub	A video format where creators lip-sync to music or audio clips.
Reaction Memes	Popular memes that TikTok users respond to or react.
Video Views	The number of times a video has been watched.
Shadow ban	When a creator's videos are restricted or receive fewer views without a formal ban.
Trending Filters	Visual effects that are currently popular across the platform.
Hashtag Strategy	A method used by creators to choose the most effective hashtags for maximum reach.
Content Series	A set of videos that follow a theme or story, often uploaded sequentially.

MASTER TIKTOK AND GO VIRAL!

Are you ready to take your TikTok content to the next level? Whether you're a creator looking to grow your personal brand or a business aiming to expand its digital presence, this book provides everything you need to understand TikTok and start creating viral content.

In 10 Actions to creating a Viral TikTok video, digital creator and marketing expert Nova Johansson shares her proven strategies for achieving viral success. Drawing from over three years of experiments on the platform, Nova breaks down the key elements of TikTok's algorithm, trends and content creation techniques that drive engagement.

INSIDE YOU'LL LEARN HOW TO

- Quickly identify and jump on trends before they fade.
- Leverage humor and relatability to connect with viewers.
- Use visual cues and hooks that capture attention.
- Optimize your posting strategy for consistent growth.
- Use the momentum of viral videos and keep engagement.

CONTENT CREATION BOOSTERS

Plus, every chapter comes with **Content Creation Boosters** to help you apply the lessons directly to your own TikTok journey. Start building viral videos that capture attention, spark engagement and grow your following today!

Nova Johansson is a digital marketing & ecom strategist and viral content creator with over 20 years of experience. She has generated millions of views on TikTok through her innovative strategies and deep understanding of the platform.

ISBN 9798343329162

9 798343 329162